Travel Journal

go where you feel most alive

TRAVEL *Bucket List*

PLACES I WANT TO VISIT:

THINGS I WANT TO SEE:

TOP 3 DESTINATIONS:

VACATION *Planner*

DATE OF TRIP: _____   DURATION: _____

NOTES

PACKING *Check List*

DOCUMENTS

- [ ] PASSPORT
- [ ] DRIVER'S LICENSE
- [ ] VISA
- [ ] PLANE TICKETS
- [ ] LOCAL CURRENCY
- [ ] INSURANCE CARD
- [ ] HEALTH CARD
- [ ] OTHER ID
- [ ] HOTEL INFORMATION
- [ ] _____

CLOTHING

- [ ] UNDERWEAR / SOCKS
- [ ] SWIM WEAR
- [ ] T-SHIRTS
- [ ] JEANS/PANTS
- [ ] SHORTS
- [ ] SKIRTS / DRESSES
- [ ] JACKET / COAT
- [ ] SLEEPWEAR
- [ ] SHOES
- [ ] _____

PERSONAL ITEMS

- [ ] SHAMPOO
- [ ] RAZORS
- [ ] COSMETICS
- [ ] HAIR BRUSH
- [ ] LIP BALM
- [ ] WATER BOTTLE
- [ ] SOAP
- [ ] TOOTHBRUSH
- [ ] JEWELRY
- [ ] _____

ELECTRONICS

- [ ] CELL PHONE
- [ ] CHARGER
- [ ] LAPTOP
- [ ] BATTERIES
- [ ] EARPHONES
- [ ] FLASH DRIVE
- [ ] MEMORY CARD
- [ ] _____
- [ ] _____
- [ ] _____

HEALTH & SAFETY

- [ ] HAND SANITIZER
- [ ] SUNSCREEN
- [ ] VITAMIN SUPPLEMENTS
- [ ] BANDAIDS
- [ ] ADVIL/TYLENOL
- [ ] CONTACTS / GLASSES
- [ ] COLD/FLU MEDS
- [ ] _____
- [ ] _____
- [ ] _____

OTHER ESSENTIALS

- [ ] _____
- [ ] _____
- [ ] _____
- [ ] _____
- [ ] _____
- [ ] _____
- [ ] _____
- [ ] _____
- [ ] _____
- [ ] _____

VACATION *Planner*

DAILY ITINERARY

DATE: ....

LOCATION: ....

BUDGET: ....

TOP ACTIVITIES

MEAL PLANNER

TIME: SCHEDULE:

EXPENSES

TOTAL COST: ....

NOTES:

TRAVEL *Information*

DESTINATION: DATE:

PLACES TO STAY

THINGS TO SEE

WHERE TO EAT

RECOMMENDATIONS

FLIGHT *Information*

DATE: _____   DESTINATION: _____

AIRLINE:	
BOOKING NUMBER:	
DEPARTURE DATE:	
BOARDING TIME:	
GATE NUMBER:	
SEAT NUMBER:	
FLIGHT DURATION:	
ARRIVAL / LANDING TIME:	

DATE: _____   DESTINATION: _____

AIRLINE:	
BOOKING NUMBER:	
DEPARTURE DATE:	
BOARDING TIME:	
GATE NUMBER:	
SEAT NUMBER:	
FLIGHT DURATION:	
ARRIVAL / LANDING TIME:	

TRIP BUDGET *Planner*

DESTINATION: _____

AMOUNT NEEDED: _____

OUR GOAL DATE:

DEPOSIT TRACKER

AMOUNT DEPOSITED: **DATE DEPOSITED:**

TRIP BUDGET *Planner*

DESTINATION:

AMOUNT NEEDED:

OUR GOAL DATE:

DEPOSIT TRACKER

AMOUNT DEPOSITED: **DATE DEPOSITED:**

TRIP BUDGET *Planner*

DESTINATION: _____

AMOUNT NEEDED: _____

OUR GOAL DATE:

DEPOSIT TRACKER

AMOUNT DEPOSITED: **DATE DEPOSITED:**

TRAVEL *Information*

HOTEL INFORMATION

NAME OF HOTEL:

ADDRESS:

PHONE NUMBER:

CONFIRMATION #:

RATE PER NIGHT:

FLIGHT INFORMATION

AIRLINE:

LOCATION:

FLIGHT #:

CHECK IN TIME:

DEPARTURE TIME:

REFERENCE #:

NOTES

TRAVEL *Information*

CAR RENTAL INFORMATION

COMPANY:

ADDRESS:

PHONE NUMBER:

CONFIRMATION #:

TOTAL COST:

EVENT INFORMATION

EVENT NAME:

LOCATION:

PHONE NUMBER:

START TIME:

OTHER:

NOTES

TRIP TO DO *List*

TRIP TO DO *List*

OUTFIT *Planner*

DAY:	DESTINATION:	PACKED:	☐

DAY:

ACTIVITY:

OUTFIT:

SHOES:

ACC:

EVENING:

DAY:	DESTINATION:	PACKED:	☐

DAY:

ACTIVITY:

OUTFIT:

SHOES:

ACC:

EVENING:

DAY:	DESTINATION:	PACKED:	☐

DAY:

ACTIVITY:

OUTFIT:

SHOES:

ACC:

EVENING:

PACKING *Check List*

DATE OF TRIP: _____   DURATION: _____

PACKING *Check List*

DATE OF TRIP: _____ DURATION: _____

TRAVEL EXPENSE *Tracker*

DESTINATION: _____   BUDGET GOAL: _____

DATE:	DESCRIPTION:	CURRENCY:	AMOUNT:

TOTAL EXPENSES:

TRAVEL EXPENSE *Tracker*

DESTINATION: _____   BUDGET GOAL: _____

DATE:	DESCRIPTION:	CURRENCY:	AMOUNT:
		TOTAL EXPENSES:	

TRAVEL *Planner*

DAY:

NOTES

6

7

8

9

10

11

12

1

2

3

4

5

6

7

8

9

10

11

12

REMINDERS

TRAVEL *Journal*

TRAVEL *Planner*

PRE-TRAVEL CHECKLIST

1 MONTH BEFORE

- [ ] _____
- [ ] _____
- [ ] _____
- [ ] _____
- [ ] _____

2 WEEKS BEFORE

- [ ] _____
- [ ] _____
- [ ] _____
- [ ] _____
- [ ] _____

1 WEEK BEFORE

- [ ] _____
- [ ] _____
- [ ] _____
- [ ] _____

2 DAYS BEFORE

- [ ] _____
- [ ] _____
- [ ] _____
- [ ] _____

24 HOURS BEFORE

- [ ] _____
- [ ] _____
- [ ] _____
- [ ] _____

DAY OF TRAVEL

- [ ] _____
- [ ] _____
- [ ] _____
- [ ] _____

TRAVEL *Organizer*

DATE: LOCATION:

DATE: LOCATION:

DAY TRAVEL *Planner*

DATE:	ATTRACTION:	THINGS TO SEE

DATE:	ATTRACTION:	THINGS TO SEE

TRAVEL *Planner*

DESTINATION:

DATES:

BUDGET:

WEATHER:

CURRENCY EXCHANGE:

ACCOMODATION OVERVIEW

NAME:	LOCATION:	DATE:	ADDRESS:

NOTES & TRAVEL DETAILS

DAILY TRAVEL *Planner*

MON

TUE

WED

THU

DAILY TRAVEL *Planner*

FRI

SAT

SUN

TRAVEL EXPENSE *Tracker*

TRIP DURATION: _____   BUDGET GOAL: _____

DATE:	DESCRIPTION:	CURRENCY:

TRAVEL *Itinerary*

DESTINATION: DATE:

MON

TUE

WED

THU

FRI

SAT

SUN

TRAVEL *Tracker*

DAILY ITINERARY

DATE: ....

LOCATION: ....

BUDGET: ....

TOP ACTIVITIES

MEAL PLANNER

TIME: SCHEDULE:

EXPENSES

....

....

....

....

TOTAL COST: ....

NOTES:

Bon Voyage

VACATION *Planner*

DATE OF TRIP: _____   DURATION: _____

NOTES

TRAVEL *Bucket List*

PLACES I WANT TO VISIT:

THINGS I WANT TO SEE:

TOP 3 DESTINATIONS:

VACATION *Planner*

DATE OF TRIP: _____   DURATION: _____

_____	_____
_____	_____
_____	_____
_____	_____
_____	_____
_____	_____
_____	_____
_____	_____
_____	_____
_____	_____
_____	_____
_____	_____
_____	_____
_____	_____
_____	_____
_____	_____
_____	_____

NOTES

PACKING *Check List*

DOCUMENTS

- ☐ PASSPORT
- ☐ DRIVER'S LICENSE
- ☐ VISA
- ☐ PLANE TICKETS
- ☐ LOCAL CURRENCY
- ☐ INSURANCE CARD
- ☐ HEALTH CARD
- ☐ OTHER ID
- ☐ HOTEL INFORMATION
- ☐ _____

CLOTHING

- ☐ UNDERWEAR / SOCKS
- ☐ SWIM WEAR
- ☐ T-SHIRTS
- ☐ JEANS/PANTS
- ☐ SHORTS
- ☐ SKIRTS / DRESSES
- ☐ JACKET / COAT
- ☐ SLEEPWEAR
- ☐ SHOES
- ☐ _____

PERSONAL ITEMS

- ☐ SHAMPOO
- ☐ RAZORS
- ☐ COSMETICS
- ☐ HAIR BRUSH
- ☐ LIP BALM
- ☐ WATER BOTTLE
- ☐ SOAP
- ☐ TOOTHBRUSH
- ☐ JEWELRY
- ☐ _____

ELECTRONICS

- ☐ CELL PHONE
- ☐ CHARGER
- ☐ LAPTOP
- ☐ BATTERIES
- ☐ EARPHONES
- ☐ FLASH DRIVE
- ☐ MEMORY CARD
- ☐ _____
- ☐ _____
- ☐ _____

HEALTH & SAFETY

- ☐ HAND SANITIZER
- ☐ SUNSCREEN
- ☐ VITAMIN SUPPLEMENTS
- ☐ BANDAIDS
- ☐ ADVIL/TYLENOL
- ☐ CONTACTS / GLASSES
- ☐ COLD/FLU MEDS
- ☐ _____
- ☐ _____
- ☐ _____

OTHER ESSENTIALS

- ☐ _____
- ☐ _____
- ☐ _____
- ☐ _____
- ☐ _____
- ☐ _____
- ☐ _____
- ☐ _____
- ☐ _____
- ☐ _____

VACATION *Planner*

DAILY ITINERARY

DATE: ....

LOCATION: ....

BUDGET: ....

TOP ACTIVITIES

MEAL PLANNER

TIME:	SCHEDULE:

EXPENSES

....

.... | ....

.... | ....

.... | ....

.... | ....

.... | ....

TOTAL COST: ....

NOTES:

TRAVEL *Information*

DESTINATION: **DATE:**

PLACES TO STAY

THINGS TO SEE

WHERE TO EAT

RECOMMENDATIONS

FLIGHT *Information*

DATE: _____   DESTINATION: _____

AIRLINE:	
BOOKING NUMBER:	
DEPARTURE DATE:	
BOARDING TIME:	
GATE NUMBER:	
SEAT NUMBER:	
FLIGHT DURATION	
ARRIVAL / LANDING TIME:	

DATE: _____   DESTINATION: _____

AIRLINE:	
BOOKING NUMBER:	
DEPARTURE DATE:	
BOARDING TIME:	
GATE NUMBER:	
SEAT NUMBER:	
FLIGHT DURATION	
ARRIVAL / LANDING TIME:	

TRIP BUDGET *Planner*

DESTINATION: _____

AMOUNT NEEDED: _____

OUR GOAL DATE:

DEPOSIT TRACKER

AMOUNT DEPOSITED: **DATE DEPOSITED:**

TRIP BUDGET *Planner*

DESTINATION:

AMOUNT NEEDED:

OUR GOAL DATE:

DEPOSIT TRACKER

AMOUNT DEPOSITED: **DATE DEPOSITED:**

TRIP BUDGET *Planner*

DESTINATION: _____

AMOUNT NEEDED: _____

OUR GOAL DATE:

DEPOSIT TRACKER

AMOUNT DEPOSITED: **DATE DEPOSITED:**

TRAVEL *Information*

HOTEL INFORMATION

NAME OF HOTEL:

ADDRESS:

PHONE NUMBER:

CONFIRMATION #:

RATE PER NIGHT:

FLIGHT INFORMATION

AIRLINE:

LOCATION:

FLIGHT #:

CHECK IN TIME:

DEPARTURE TIME:

REFERENCE #:

NOTES

TRAVEL *Information*

<table>
<tr><td rowspan="6">CAR RENTAL INFORMATION</td><td>COMPANY:</td><td></td></tr>
<tr><td>ADDRESS:</td><td></td></tr>
<tr><td>PHONE NUMBER:</td><td></td></tr>
<tr><td>CONFIRMATION #:</td><td></td></tr>
<tr><td>TOTAL COST:</td><td></td></tr>
</table>

<table>
<tr><td rowspan="5">EVENT INFORMATION</td><td>EVENT NAME:</td><td></td></tr>
<tr><td>LOCATION:</td><td></td></tr>
<tr><td>PHONE NUMBER:</td><td></td></tr>
<tr><td>START TIME:</td><td></td></tr>
<tr><td>OTHER:</td><td></td></tr>
</table>

NOTES

TRIP TO DO *List*

☐

☐

☐

☐

☐

☐

☐

☐

☐

TRIP TO DO *List*

OUTFIT *Planner*

DAY:	DESTINATION:	PACKED: ☐

DAY:

EVENING:

ACTIVITY:

OUTFIT:

SHOES:

ACC:

DAY:	DESTINATION:	PACKED: ☐

DAY:

EVENING:

ACTIVITY:

OUTFIT:

SHOES:

ACC:

DAY:	DESTINATION:	PACKED: ☐

DAY:

EVENING:

ACTIVITY:

OUTFIT:

SHOES:

ACC:

PACKING *Check List*

DATE OF TRIP: _____   DURATION: _____

PACKING *Check List*

DATE OF TRIP: _____   DURATION: _____

TRAVEL EXPENSE *Tracker*

DESTINATION: _____   BUDGET GOAL: _____

DATE:	DESCRIPTION:	CURRENCY:	AMOUNT:

	TOTAL EXPENSES:

TRAVEL EXPENSE *Tracker*

DESTINATION: _____   BUDGET GOAL: _____

DATE:	DESCRIPTION:	CURRENCY:	AMOUNT:

TOTAL EXPENSES:

TRAVEL *Planner*

DATE:

☀ 🌤 🌦 ☁ ⛈

6	
7	
8	
9	
10	
11	
12	
1	
2	
3	
4	
5	
6	
7	
8	
9	
10	
11	
12	

DAY:

NOTES

REMINDERS

TRAVEL *Journal*

TRAVEL *Planner*

PRE-TRAVEL CHECKLIST

1 MONTH BEFORE

- [ ]
- [ ]
- [ ]
- [ ]
- [ ]

2 WEEKS BEFORE

- [ ]
- [ ]
- [ ]
- [ ]
- [ ]

1 WEEK BEFORE

- [ ]
- [ ]
- [ ]
- [ ]
- [ ]

2 DAYS BEFORE

- [ ]
- [ ]
- [ ]
- [ ]
- [ ]

24 HOURS BEFORE

- [ ]
- [ ]
- [ ]
- [ ]
- [ ]

DAY OF TRAVEL

- [ ]
- [ ]
- [ ]
- [ ]
- [ ]

TRAVEL *Organizer*

DATE: **LOCATION:**

DATE: **LOCATION:**

DAY TRAVEL *Planner*

DATE:	ATTRACTION:

THINGS TO SEE

- _____
- _____
- _____
- _____
- _____
- _____
- _____
- _____
- _____
- _____

DATE:	ATTRACTION:

THINGS TO SEE

- _____
- _____
- _____
- _____
- _____
- _____
- _____
- _____
- _____
- _____

TRAVEL *Planner*

DESTINATION:	DATES:

BUDGET:	WEATHER:	CURRENCY EXCHANGE:

ACCOMODATION OVERVIEW

NAME:	LOCATION:	DATE:	ADDRESS:

NOTES & TRAVEL DETAILS

DAILY TRAVEL *Planner*

MON

TUE

WED

THU

DAILY TRAVEL *Planner*

FRI

SAT

SUN

TRAVEL EXPENSE *Tracker*

TRIP DURATION: _____   BUDGET GOAL: _____

DATE:	DESCRIPTION:	CURRENCY:

TRAVEL *Itinerary*

DESTINATION: DATE:

MON

TUE

WED

THU

FRI

SAT

SUN

TRAVEL *Tracker*

DAILY ITINERARY

DATE: ....

LOCATION: ....

BUDGET: ....

TOP ACTIVITIES

MEAL PLANNER

TIME: SCHEDULE:

EXPENSES

....

....

....

....

....

TOTAL COST: ....

NOTES:

Bon Voyage

Enjoy every moment

VACATION *Planner*

DATE OF TRIP: _____   DURATION: _____

NOTES

TRAVEL *Bucket List*

PLACES I WANT TO VISIT:

_____
_____
_____
_____
_____
_____
_____
_____
_____
_____

THINGS I WANT TO SEE:

_____
_____
_____
_____
_____
_____
_____
_____
_____
_____
_____
_____
_____
_____
_____

TOP 3 DESTINATIONS:

_____
_____
_____

VACATION *Planner*

DATE OF TRIP: _____   DURATION: _____

- [ ] _____   - [ ] _____
- [ ] _____   - [ ] _____
- [ ] _____   - [ ] _____
- [ ] _____   - [ ] _____
- [ ] _____   - [ ] _____
- [ ] _____   - [ ] _____
- [ ] _____   - [ ] _____
- [ ] _____   - [ ] _____
- [ ] _____   - [ ] _____
- [ ] _____   - [ ] _____
- [ ] _____   - [ ] _____
- [ ] _____   - [ ] _____
- [ ] _____   - [ ] _____
- [ ] _____   - [ ] _____
- [ ] _____   - [ ] _____
- [ ] _____   - [ ] _____
- [ ] _____   - [ ] _____
- [ ] _____   - [ ] _____

NOTES

PACKING *Check List*

DOCUMENTS

- ☐ PASSPORT
- ☐ DRIVER'S LICENSE
- ☐ VISA
- ☐ PLANE TICKETS
- ☐ LOCAL CURRENCY
- ☐ INSURANCE CARD
- ☐ HEALTH CARD
- ☐ OTHER ID
- ☐ HOTEL INFORMATION
- ☐ _____

CLOTHING

- ☐ UNDERWEAR / SOCKS
- ☐ SWIM WEAR
- ☐ T-SHIRTS
- ☐ JEANS/PANTS
- ☐ SHORTS
- ☐ SKIRTS / DRESSES
- ☐ JACKET / COAT
- ☐ SLEEPWEAR
- ☐ SHOES
- ☐ _____

PERSONAL ITEMS

- ☐ SHAMPOO
- ☐ RAZORS
- ☐ COSMETICS
- ☐ HAIR BRUSH
- ☐ LIP BALM
- ☐ WATER BOTTLE
- ☐ SOAP
- ☐ TOOTHBRUSH
- ☐ JEWELRY
- ☐ _____

ELECTRONICS

- ☐ CELL PHONE
- ☐ CHARGER
- ☐ LAPTOP
- ☐ BATTERIES
- ☐ EARPHONES
- ☐ FLASH DRIVE
- ☐ MEMORY CARD
- ☐ _____
- ☐ _____
- ☐ _____

HEALTH & SAFETY

- ☐ HAND SANITIZER
- ☐ SUNSCREEN
- ☐ VITAMIN SUPPLEMENTS
- ☐ BANDAIDS
- ☐ ADVIL/TYLENOL
- ☐ CONTACTS / GLASSES
- ☐ COLD/FLU MEDS
- ☐ _____
- ☐ _____
- ☐ _____

OTHER ESSENTIALS

- ☐ _____
- ☐ _____
- ☐ _____
- ☐ _____
- ☐ _____
- ☐ _____
- ☐ _____
- ☐ _____
- ☐ _____
- ☐ _____

VACATION *Planner*

DAILY ITINERARY

DATE: ....

LOCATION: ....

BUDGET: ....

☼ ⛅ 🌦 ☁ ⛈

MEAL PLANNER

EXPENSES

....

....

....

....

....

TOTAL COST: ....

TOP ACTIVITIES

TIME:	SCHEDULE:

NOTES:

TRAVEL *Information*

DESTINATION: **DATE:**

PLACES TO STAY

THINGS TO SEE

WHERE TO EAT

RECOMMENDATIONS

FLIGHT *Information*

DATE: _____ DESTINATION: _____

AIRLINE:	
BOOKING NUMBER:	
DEPARTURE DATE:	
BOARDING TIME:	
GATE NUMBER:	
SEAT NUMBER:	
FLIGHT DURATION:	
ARRIVAL / LANDING TIME:	

DATE: _____ DESTINATION: _____

AIRLINE:	
BOOKING NUMBER:	
DEPARTURE DATE:	
BOARDING TIME:	
GATE NUMBER:	
SEAT NUMBER:	
FLIGHT DURATION:	
ARRIVAL / LANDING TIME:	

TRIP BUDGET *Planner*

DESTINATION: _____

AMOUNT NEEDED: _____

OUR GOAL DATE: _____

DEPOSIT TRACKER

AMOUNT DEPOSITED: **DATE DEPOSITED:**

TRIP BUDGET *Planner*

DESTINATION: _____

AMOUNT NEEDED: _____

OUR GOAL DATE:

DEPOSIT TRACKER

AMOUNT DEPOSITED: **DATE DEPOSITED:**

TRIP BUDGET *Planner*

DESTINATION:

AMOUNT NEEDED:

OUR GOAL DATE:

DEPOSIT TRACKER

AMOUNT DEPOSITED: **DATE DEPOSITED:**

TRAVEL *Information*

HOTEL INFORMATION

NAME OF HOTEL:

ADDRESS:

PHONE NUMBER:

CONFIRMATION #:

RATE PER NIGHT:

FLIGHT INFORMATION

AIRLINE:

LOCATION:

FLIGHT #:

CHECK IN TIME:

DEPARTURE TIME:

REFERENCE #:

NOTES

TRAVEL *Information*

CAR RENTAL INFORMATION

COMPANY:

ADDRESS:

PHONE NUMBER:

CONFIRMATION #:

TOTAL COST:

EVENT INFORMATION

EVENT NAME:

LOCATION:

PHONE NUMBER:

START TIME:

OTHER:

NOTES

TRIP TO DO *List*

TRIP TO DO *List*

OUTFIT *Planner*

| DAY: | DESTINATION: | PACKED: | ☐ |

| DAY: | EVENING: |

ACTIVITY: _____

OUTFIT: _____

SHOES: _____

ACC: _____

| DAY: | DESTINATION: | PACKED: | ☐ |

| DAY: | EVENING: |

ACTIVITY: _____

OUTFIT: _____

SHOES: _____

ACC: _____

| DAY: | DESTINATION: | PACKED: | ☐ |

| DAY: | EVENING: |

ACTIVITY: _____

OUTFIT: _____

SHOES: _____

ACC: _____

PACKING *Check List*

DATE OF TRIP: _____   DURATION: _____

PACKING *Check List*

DATE OF TRIP: _____   DURATION: _____

TRAVEL EXPENSE *Tracker*

DESTINATION: _____   BUDGET GOAL: _____

DATE:	DESCRIPTION:	CURRENCY:	AMOUNT:

	TOTAL EXPENSES:

TRAVEL EXPENSE *Tracker*

DESTINATION: _____   BUDGET GOAL: _____

DATE:	DESCRIPTION:	CURRENCY:	AMOUNT:

	TOTAL EXPENSES:

TRAVEL *Planner*

DAY:

NOTES

6

7

8

9

10

11

12

1

2

3

4

REMINDERS

5

6

7

8

9

10

11

12

TRAVEL *Journal*

TRAVEL *Planner*

PRE-TRAVEL CHECKLIST

1 MONTH BEFORE

- ☐ _____
- ☐ _____
- ☐ _____
- ☐ _____
- ☐ _____

2 WEEKS BEFORE

- ☐ _____
- ☐ _____
- ☐ _____
- ☐ _____
- ☐ _____

1 WEEK BEFORE

- ☐ _____
- ☐ _____
- ☐ _____
- ☐ _____
- ☐ _____

2 DAYS BEFORE

- ☐ _____
- ☐ _____
- ☐ _____
- ☐ _____
- ☐ _____

24 HOURS BEFORE

- ☐ _____
- ☐ _____
- ☐ _____
- ☐ _____
- ☐ _____

DAY OF TRAVEL

- ☐ _____
- ☐ _____
- ☐ _____
- ☐ _____
- ☐ _____

TRAVEL *Organizer*

DATE: **LOCATION:**

DATE: **LOCATION:**

DAY TRAVEL *Planner*

DATE:	ATTRACTION:

THINGS TO SEE

DATE:	ATTRACTION:

THINGS TO SEE

TRAVEL *Planner*

DESTINATION:	DATES:

BUDGET:	WEATHER:	CURRENCY EXCHANGE:

ACCOMODATION OVERVIEW

NAME:	LOCATION:	DATE:	ADDRESS:

NOTES & TRAVEL DETAILS

DAILY TRAVEL *Planner*

MON

TUE

WED

THU

DAILY TRAVEL *Planner*

FRI

SAT

SUN

never STOP exploring

TRAVEL EXPENSE *Tracker*

TRIP DURATION: _____   BUDGET GOAL: _____

DATE:	DESCRIPTION:	CURRENCY:

TRAVEL *Itinerary*

DESTINATION: DATE:

MON

TUE

WED

THU

FRI

SAT

SUN

TRAVEL *Tracker*

DAILY ITINERARY

DATE: _____

LOCATION: _____

BUDGET: _____

TOP ACTIVITIES

MEAL PLANNER

TIME:	SCHEDULE:

EXPENSES

_____   _____

_____   _____

_____   _____

_____   _____

TOTAL COST: _____

NOTES:

Bon
Voyage

VACATION *Planner*

DATE OF TRIP: _____   DURATION: _____

- [ ] _____
- [ ] _____
- [ ] _____
- [ ] _____
- [ ] _____
- [ ] _____
- [ ] _____
- [ ] _____
- [ ] _____
- [ ] _____
- [ ] _____
- [ ] _____
- [ ] _____
- [ ] _____
- [ ] _____
- [ ] _____
- [ ] _____
- [ ] _____

- [ ] _____
- [ ] _____
- [ ] _____
- [ ] _____
- [ ] _____
- [ ] _____
- [ ] _____
- [ ] _____
- [ ] _____
- [ ] _____
- [ ] _____
- [ ] _____
- [ ] _____
- [ ] _____
- [ ] _____
- [ ] _____
- [ ] _____
- [ ] _____

NOTES

TRAVEL *Bucket List*

PLACES I WANT TO VISIT:

THINGS I WANT TO SEE:

TOP 3 DESTINATIONS:

VACATION *Planner*

DATE OF TRIP: _____   DURATION: _____

☐ _____   ☐ _____
☐ _____   ☐ _____
☐ _____   ☐ _____
☐ _____   ☐ _____
☐ _____   ☐ _____
☐ _____   ☐ _____
☐ _____   ☐ _____
☐ _____   ☐ _____
☐ _____   ☐ _____
☐ _____   ☐ _____
☐ _____   ☐ _____
☐ _____   ☐ _____
☐ _____   ☐ _____
☐ _____   ☐ _____
☐ _____   ☐ _____
☐ _____   ☐ _____
☐ _____   ☐ _____
☐ _____   ☐ _____

NOTES

PACKING *Check List*

DOCUMENTS

- ☐ PASSPORT
- ☐ DRIVER'S LICENSE
- ☐ VISA
- ☐ PLANE TICKETS
- ☐ LOCAL CURRENCY
- ☐ INSURANCE CARD
- ☐ HEALTH CARD
- ☐ OTHER ID
- ☐ HOTEL INFORMATION
- ☐ _____

CLOTHING

- ☐ UNDERWEAR / SOCKS
- ☐ SWIM WEAR
- ☐ T-SHIRTS
- ☐ JEANS/PANTS
- ☐ SHORTS
- ☐ SKIRTS / DRESSES
- ☐ JACKET / COAT
- ☐ SLEEPWEAR
- ☐ SHOES
- ☐ _____

PERSONAL ITEMS

- ☐ SHAMPOO
- ☐ RAZORS
- ☐ COSMETICS
- ☐ HAIR BRUSH
- ☐ LIP BALM
- ☐ WATER BOTTLE
- ☐ SOAP
- ☐ TOOTHBRUSH
- ☐ JEWELRY
- ☐ _____

ELECTRONICS

- ☐ CELL PHONE
- ☐ CHARGER
- ☐ LAPTOP
- ☐ BATTERIES
- ☐ EARPHONES
- ☐ FLASH DRIVE
- ☐ MEMORY CARD
- ☐ _____
- ☐ _____
- ☐ _____

HEALTH & SAFETY

- ☐ HAND SANITIZER
- ☐ SUNSCREEN
- ☐ VITAMIN SUPPLEMENTS
- ☐ BANDAIDS
- ☐ ADVIL/TYLENOL
- ☐ CONTACTS / GLASSES
- ☐ COLD/FLU MEDS
- ☐ _____
- ☐ _____
- ☐ _____

OTHER ESSENTIALS

- ☐ _____
- ☐ _____
- ☐ _____
- ☐ _____
- ☐ _____
- ☐ _____
- ☐ _____
- ☐ _____
- ☐ _____
- ☐ _____

VACATION *Planner*

DAILY ITINERARY

DATE: ....

LOCATION: ....

BUDGET: ....

TOP ACTIVITIES

MEAL PLANNER

TIME: SCHEDULE:

EXPENSES

_____   _____

_____   _____

_____   _____

_____   _____

TOTAL COST:

NOTES:

TRAVEL *Information*

DESTINATION: DATE:

PLACES TO STAY

THINGS TO SEE

WHERE TO EAT

RECOMMENDATIONS

FLIGHT *Information*

DATE: _____   DESTINATION: _____

AIRLINE:	
BOOKING NUMBER:	
DEPARTURE DATE:	
BOARDING TIME:	
GATE NUMBER:	
SEAT NUMBER:	
FLIGHT DURATION:	
ARRIVAL / LANDING TIME:	

DATE: _____   DESTINATION: _____

AIRLINE:	
BOOKING NUMBER:	
DEPARTURE DATE:	
BOARDING TIME:	
GATE NUMBER:	
SEAT NUMBER:	
FLIGHT DURATION:	
ARRIVAL / LANDING TIME:	

TRIP BUDGET *Planner*

DESTINATION: _____

AMOUNT NEEDED: _____

OUR GOAL DATE:

DEPOSIT TRACKER

AMOUNT DEPOSITED: **DATE DEPOSITED:**

TRIP BUDGET *Planner*

DESTINATION: _____

AMOUNT NEEDED: _____

OUR GOAL DATE: [   ]

DEPOSIT TRACKER

AMOUNT DEPOSITED:	DATE DEPOSITED:

TRIP BUDGET *Planner*

DESTINATION:

AMOUNT NEEDED:

OUR GOAL DATE:

DEPOSIT TRACKER

AMOUNT DEPOSITED:

DATE DEPOSITED:

TRAVEL *Information*

HOTEL INFORMATION

NAME OF HOTEL:

ADDRESS:

PHONE NUMBER:

CONFIRMATION #:

RATE PER NIGHT:

FLIGHT INFORMATION

AIRLINE:

LOCATION:

FLIGHT #:

CHECK IN TIME:

DEPARTURE TIME:

REFERENCE #:

NOTES

TRAVEL *Information*

CAR RENTAL INFORMATION

COMPANY:

ADDRESS:

PHONE NUMBER:

CONFIRMATION #:

TOTAL COST:

EVENT INFORMATION

EVENT NAME:

LOCATION:

PHONE NUMBER:

START TIME:

OTHER:

NOTES

TRIP TO DO *List*

TRIP TO DO *List*

- [ ]
- [ ]
- [ ]
- [ ]
- [ ]
- [ ]
- [ ]
- [ ]
- [ ]

OUTFIT *Planner*

DAY: **DESTINATION:**   **PACKED:** ☐

DAY:	**EVENING:**
ACTIVITY: _____	
OUTFIT: _____	
SHOES: _____	
ACC: _____	

DAY: **DESTINATION:**   **PACKED:** ☐

DAY:	**EVENING:**
ACTIVITY: _____	
OUTFIT: _____	
SHOES: _____	
ACC: _____	

DAY: **DESTINATION:**   **PACKED:** ☐

DAY:	**EVENING:**
ACTIVITY: _____	
OUTFIT: _____	
SHOES: _____	
ACC: _____	

PACKING *Check List*

DATE OF TRIP: _____   DURATION: _____

PACKING *Check List*

DATE OF TRIP: _____   DURATION: _____

TRAVEL EXPENSE *Tracker*

DESTINATION: _____   BUDGET GOAL: _____

DATE:	DESCRIPTION:	CURRENCY:	AMOUNT:

	TOTAL EXPENSES:

TRAVEL EXPENSE *Tracker*

DESTINATION: _____   BUDGET GOAL: _____

DATE:	DESCRIPTION:	CURRENCY:	AMOUNT:

TOTAL EXPENSES:

TRAVEL *Planner*

DATE:

DAY:

☀ ⛅ 🌦 ☁ ⛈

6

7

8

9

10

11

12

1

2

3

4

5

6

7

8

9

10

11

12

NOTES

REMINDERS

TRAVEL *Journal*

TRAVEL *Planner*

PRE-TRAVEL CHECKLIST

1 MONTH BEFORE	2 WEEKS BEFORE

☐ _____ ☐ _____

☐ _____ ☐ _____

☐ _____ ☐ _____

☐ _____ ☐ _____

☐ _____ ☐ _____

1 WEEK BEFORE	2 DAYS BEFORE

☐ _____ ☐ _____

☐ _____ ☐ _____

☐ _____ ☐ _____

☐ _____ ☐ _____

☐ _____ ☐ _____

24 HOURS BEFORE	DAY OF TRAVEL

☐ _____ ☐ _____

☐ _____ ☐ _____

☐ _____ ☐ _____

☐ _____ ☐ _____

☐ _____ ☐ _____

TRAVEL *Organizer*

DATE: LOCATION:

DATE: LOCATION:

DAY TRAVEL *Planner*

DATE:	ATTRACTION:

THINGS TO SEE

DATE:	ATTRACTION:

THINGS TO SEE

TRAVEL *Planner*

DESTINATION:

DATES:

BUDGET:

WEATHER:

CURRENCY EXCHANGE:

ACCOMODATION OVERVIEW

NAME:	LOCATION:	DATE:	ADDRESS:

NOTES & TRAVEL DETAILS

DAILY TRAVEL *Planner*

MON

TUE

WED

THU

DAILY TRAVEL *Planner*

FRI

SAT

SUN

never STOP exploring

TRAVEL EXPENSE *Tracker*

TRIP DURATION: _____   BUDGET GOAL: _____

DATE:	DESCRIPTION:	CURRENCY:

TRAVEL *Itinerary*

DESTINATION: DATE:

MON

TUE

WED

THU

FRI

SAT

SUN

TRAVEL *Tracker*

DAILY ITINERARY

DATE: ....

LOCATION: ....

BUDGET: ....

TOP ACTIVITIES

MEAL PLANNER

TIME: SCHEDULE:

EXPENSES

....

....

....

....

TOTAL COST: ....

NOTES:

travel is always a good IDEA

If you have any questions, requests or suggestions, feel free to write to us at the e-mail address below.
If you liked the planner, we would be grateful for a short review.
We know that it takes a moment and is often considered unnecessary, but you could help our small business and potential customers enormously with it.
Best regards

Maximus Designs

Legal Notice / Impressum
Copyright: Maximus Designs 2019
E-Mail: Shirtdesignerz@yahoo.com
Cover, translation and design by Maximilian Klein,Goldammerstr.18,12351 Berlin, Germany

46202505R00085

Printed in Poland
by Amazon Fulfillment
Poland Sp. z o.o., Wrocław